Whose M[ind] Is It Anyway?

Get Out of Your Head and Into Your Life

Lisa and Franco Esile

A TarcherPerigee Book

tarcherperigee

An imprint of Penguin Random House LLC

375 Hudson Street, New York, New York 10014

Copyright © 2016 by Lisa Esile and Franco Esile

Most TarcherPerigee books are available at special quantity discounts for bulk purchases for sales promotions, premiums, fund-raising, or educational use. Special books, or book excerpts, can also be created to fit specific needs. For details, write: SpecialMarkets@penguinrandomhouse.com.

ISBN: 978-1-101-98263-1

PRINTED IN THE UNITED STATES OF AMERICA

5 7 9 10 8 6 4

To You

Maybe you're reading this book because you like books about the mind.

Or because you like to read 100 books a year and you heard this was a short one.

Maybe your life is going REALLY well, and you're at a friend's place and you found this in their reading room.

There's something you should know.

Feeling unhappy and out of sorts is a sure sign you've been hoodwinked by your mind.

Yes!

It's also the PERFECT time for learning stuff that'll make your life better than ever.

Because there are things our mind is GOOD at and things it's NOT.

And knowing which is which can make life a whole lot easier.

A few words about this book:

There's NO homework

This book shows you how to see you're already ok by looking at things in a different way. So you don't really have to DO anything.

We didn't make this stuff up

For thousands of years people have written about how this whole "being human" thing works.

Often with less pictures. And jokes. And usually a lot more words.

This book boils down universal truths into usable, easy-to-grasp nuggets. It reveals 7 common (but unhelpful) beliefs that keep us from feeling ok.

So, without further ado:

Here are 7 ways your mind tricks you out of feeling peaceful and what you can do about it.

wisdom

YOUR MIND THINKS ...

I am SO wise.

WHEN REALLY ...

Your mind isn't wise at all.

From an early age we're taught:

Listen to your mind
above all else.

Reason & logic
are the way to get ahead.

Do all you can to
strengthen your mind.

We crown our mind
King
of ALL our decisions.

We, like, um, totally
LOVE the idea of how brainy we are.

With our opposable
thumbs,

toilets that self-flush,

and telephones that tell you
the song on the radio.

Our mind thinks it's the
BIGGEST BRAIN BOX
in the world.

We think we
ARE our mind.
(Which our mind really likes.)

But

Our mind isn't the only thing that helps us make sense of the world.

We also have our heart.

Yes. But my mind is the SMARTEST bit, right??

Awkward pause.

Your mind might have convinced
you it's SUPER SMART
and BRAINY

& knows everything there is
to know about everything.

But compared to your heart
your mind isn't wise at all.

You don't even have to
read this book, I already
know all this stuff.

YOUR MIND COMPUTES.
LIKE A COMPUTER.

It JUDGES everything.

It ASSUMES and OVER SIMPLIFIES.

It constantly SCANS THE PAST looking
for patterns to help predict the future.

And while computers can do
amazing things, they're not wise.

So if the mind's not wise, where does wisdom come from?

Your Wisdom lies within Your HEART

YOUR Heart
is your
intuitive Voice.

We ALL have it,
and
it ISN'T Magic.

Your Intuition isn't based on logic. And often doesn't make sense at the time. It's more

An inkling

A vague hunch

A flash of inspiration.

Think of it as a different kind of intelligence that comes from deep within & is connected to everything.

CHAPTER TWO

calm

YOUR MIND THINKS ...

I'll feel calm when I get a promotion, buy a house, and climb Mt Salvation.

WHEN REALLY ...

Want to know the
truth about
feeling calm?

Are you sure?

REALLY sure?

Because your mind probably won't like it.

OKay,
you asked for it...

You already have all the calm, relaxed, self-assured feelings you're looking for.

The same feelings you think you'd feel
if things were different.

When you don't feel calm it's because you've got a bunch of STUFF on top of your calm distracting you from it.

That
stuff
is
your
mind.

Okay, this is hard to hear sometimes, and the kind of thing that makes you want to punch the person who says it.

But at the risk of bearing one of your thought punches ...

Feeling stressed is a choice.

BLAMO

Whether you're in the curled-in-a-ball stage or you're just wandering around feeling dissatisfied, resentful, afraid, & unsure of yourself, the cause is the same:

Too much listening to your fraidy cat, over-analyzing, assumption—making, judgmental puddleweed of a mind.

YOU are calm, contented, and self-assured.

YOU *love* YOURSELF.

Even if your mind doesn't know it.

Please, please don't go judging how you feel, or trying to be something else.

It's really more helpful just to NOTICE.

And LET. IT. BE.

Okay. But my thoughts can be so overwhelming. I'd really like to stop the horrible ones.

THE GREAT GRAPE TRICK.

Imagine a BUNCH OF GRAPES sitting on your head. They are your thoughts.

When you're aware that thoughts are things that go THROUGH you, but are not YOU ... you create space.

When there is space between YOU and YOUR THOUGHTS, it's easy to see them for what they are...

Just thoughts.

Coming and going through your mind.

TRYING TO CONTROL OUR THOUGHTS IS LIKE *Lassoing* A BUCKING BRONCO MADE OF GRAPE JELLY.

It's slippery.

Sure, we can learn to control them somewhat through meditation or white-knuckle determination. But that's missing the point.

Thoughts roll in from who knows where. They roll out again.

Imagine your mind is a freight train with a thousand cars filled with thoughts.

Now, imagine yourself on top of a hill.
Your thought train is still rumbling away.
Only you're looking up at the sky.

From afar, comfy thoughts look the
same as the non-comfy ones.

It can be hard to remember that we're not our thoughts.

Keep reading.

You'll see it doesn't even matter if you forget.

And remember ...

You are
CALM.
Your mind
might not be.

Now on to the third trick our mind plays.

This one is so subversive they might not even print this part... if you see blacked out areas like this

you'll know why.

CHAPTER THREE

Control

YOUR MIND THINKS ...

I am SO carefree and easygoing.

WHEN REALLY ...

YOUR mind wants to CONTROL EVERYTHING.

Really?

Yes!

Your mind thinks it needs to control you to keep you safe from lions and flying spears. And from regrettable footwear choices.

In the name of SAFETY and CAUTION your Mind will LIMIT YOU and KEEP YOU from NEW EXPERIENCES.

It'll have you:

* Sticking with the pack when you'd rather do your own thing.

* Focusing so much on the approval of others you forget you even have your own thing.

* Avoiding unknown situations.

* Ordering the grilled cheese every time.

Left unchecked your mind will take as much control as you let it,

It can rob you of your dreams and visions.

YOUR MIND TRIES to CONTROL YOU

Trying to control the world is tiring.
It takes a lot of effort.
Not to mention it's not possible.

AND you become harder to connect with.

We have all kinds of justifications for being controlling.

But ultimately, we're concerned about the outcome for ourselves. At least our mind is.

You don't have to spend your life at the mercy of your overbearing, dream-robbing, control freak of a mind.

YOU are actually in charge.

I mean,

To be in charge isn't about trying to control your mind, it's about seeing your thoughts for what they are and not being pushed around by them.
It's about ...

Trust that you can handle whatever happens.

Trust that things will work out.

The more you do it, the easier it gets.

And you begin to see how your rules aren't always the best.

Remember how the mind isn't wise?

The more we blindly follow our mind's controlling ways, the less in touch with ourselves we are.

The less we hear our HEART.

And we miss the flow of life...

The sun shining.

People laughing.

All the cool and natural ways people do things, ways you've never even thought of.

Knowing about your mind's controlling ways is a good start.

PLAY with them.

CHALLENGE them.

Your mind says you can't go to the gym until you lose weight. What happens if you do?

Your girlfriend says you're too old to be a DJ. What happens if you go for it?

You're nervous about going to the party alone. Try it and see!

Your mind says quitting medicine to ride a unicycle in the circus (even though you want to more than anything) is ridiculous...

WHAT HAPPENS IF YOU

DO IT ANYWAY!?

CHAPTER FOUR

Learning

YOUR MIND THINKS ...

I L.O.V.E. LOVE learning!

WHEN REALLY ....

YOUR MIND
ABSO-
LUTELY,
COMP-
LETELY
DOES **NOT** WANT
to *Learn.*

and change is UNPREDICTABLE,
which can be TERRIFYING
for the mind.

Your mind will do EVERYTHING to convince you NOT to change.

It will tell you things like:

"I'm too old to change."

"I'm too young to change."

"But I've always been this way."

"People will laugh at me."

"Things aren't that bad. It's okay, really."

Your mind would rather be
UNCOMFORTABLE in a FAMILIAR
situation than

RISK something NEW.

I love cheese toast, but I've never eaten off a truck before.

Get the picture?

Your mind wants
PREDICTABILITY!

Your mind HATES
surprises!

Your mind HATES to
learn!

The need for predictability is why people repeat old habits over and over again even though they might be painful.

The need for predictability is why people repeat old habits over and over again even though they might be painful.

Painful, huh?

When you try
something new,
don't be surprised
if your mind
is reluctant.

Expect it to be.

But what about all the studying
I've done, all the books I've read?

Studying and remembering facts isn't
the kind of learning where you take on
a NEW BELIEF.

Which is exactly the type of learning
required for ACTUAL CHANGE.

Your mind loves new information. But it's only interested in the kind that supports its existing set of beliefs.

As we grow, we form BELIEFS about what we can and can't do ...

based on what teachers tell us, on what our family says, and on how we think we compare to others.

We wind up thinking:

* I'm just not creative.
* I'm such a slow reader, there's no point.
* I'm too uncoordinated for tennis.
* I'm not good at relationships.
* I'm tone-deaf. I absolutely can't sing.

These ideas become so much a part of us we think they are THE TRUTH.

But they're not!

Yeah, but you don't understand. I actually CANNOT sing.

We're belief blind.

It's like being colorblind but for beliefs. Our ability is sitting right in front of us. We just can't see it.

TAKE SINGING

Lots of people believe they can't sing, but almost everyone can find pitch and hold a note if they're shown how. People often say they're tone-deaf when they haven't really tried.

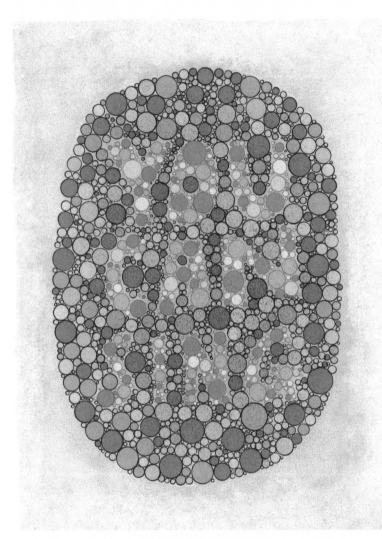

It's the same with any new belief.
They're hard to see sometimes.

What are you doing?

Writing down what some of my limiting beliefs might be so I can figure them out.

Don't do that! Well, you can if you want to. But it's more simple than that.

Start noticing how QUICK your mind is TO REJECT new ideas.

The next time you get an urge to instantly disagree or say, "I can't," pause. Put it in your ponder ball.

This is a ponder ball.

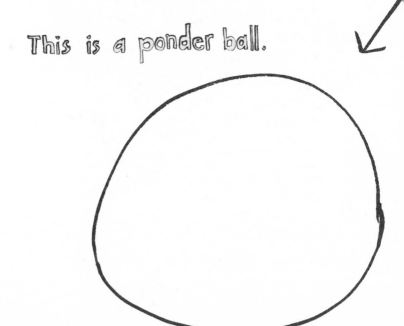

Place new ideas in here.

✓ You don't need to "think them through." Just let them roll around. See how they look in a few days or weeks. Ask yourself, is this really true?

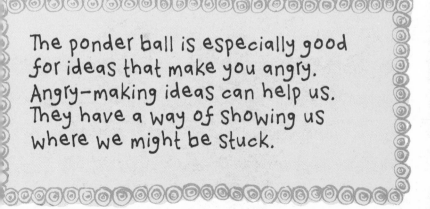

The ponder ball is especially good for ideas that make you angry. Angry-making ideas can help us. They have a way of showing us where we might be stuck.

Pay attention to deep desires. Don't worry if you'll be "good," just do it.

Take a small step.

If your mind says you're being silly or that you're going to embarrass yourself, go for it!

You're probably onto something.

CHAPTER FIVE

Pain

YOUR MIND THINKS ...

My pain and sadness are caused by bad things happening to me.

WHEN REALLY ...

Sorry about that. I've always wanted to try this.

You were saying?

Pain is what?

We think pain is what happens when people say unkind things, we experience a loss, or we trail toilet paper from our heel on a first date. But the truth is,

a lot of our pain comes from negative or faulty beliefs about how we're not good enough.

And many of our beliefs are garden variety, everyone-believes-them kinds of beliefs, making them hard to spot.

Our mind loves to collect and hold on to critical thoughts:

We compare ourselves to others.

We pick up messages at school, work, home, and from the media about how we should behave, how we should look, how we should be doing better.

And we remember times when we were reprimanded or made fun of and carry them with us.

These critical thoughts turn into faulty beliefs.

These faulty beliefs sit on top of our mind, like Band-Aids. They cover our well-being and make it hard to feel good.

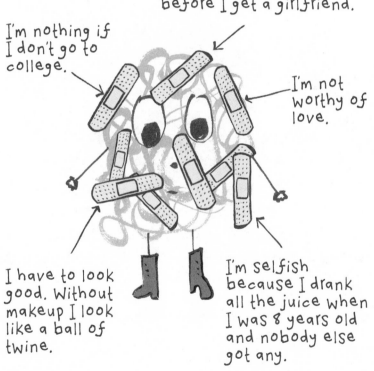

I need a better job before I get a girlfriend.

I'm nothing if I don't go to college.

I'm not worthy of love.

I have to look good. Without makeup I look like a ball of twine.

I'm selfish because I drank all the juice when I was 8 years old and nobody else got any.

The idea that we're not good enough pushes us around, in small ways, every day.

It's like this:

If someone makes fun of your ears and you like your ears, you're not going to feel too bad. But if you're insecure about your ears, you might feel upset. You might even start wearing big ear-covering hats.

It's NOT THE THING that makes us feel bad, but our THOUGHTS about THE THING.

Our mind uses these thoughts to inform our choices, creating a kind of roadmap it thinks will lead to happiness.

We move along with a mysterious certainty that things ought to be a specific way, as if we know the ideal way for life to happen.

The Universe, laughing.

ha ha
haha
ha haha
ha

And when life doesn't turn out like we planned ...

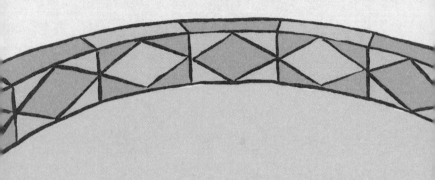

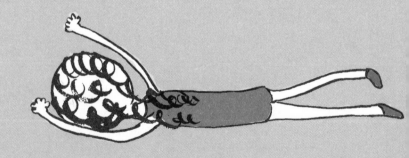

it's painful.

We feel like something large and precious has been taken away.

But it hasn't.

What we've lost is the roadmap for how we think things should play out.

Our roadmaps are so real for us, we lose sight of the fact that they're just ideas.

A plan based on a bunch of beliefs, many faulty, about how life should go.

And sometimes. . .

what feels like a roadblock is actually the doorway to a life of greater ease and joy.

It's easy to think that we shouldn't feel upset or hurt. But pain is normal and healthy.

It can be the rudder that steers us back on course. Truth is, we're more self-correcting than we realize.

Our pain is an indicator of our faulty beliefs and insecurities.

So what should I do?

How do we get rid of our faulty beliefs?

Should we hunt them down like a detective and interrogate them?

Should we assemble all our family and hand out cryptic questionnaires to flush out the culprits?

How about point a flashlight at a bowl of sudsy water and leave it on the living room floor overnight*?

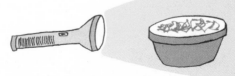

* Also good for catching fleas.

Nope!

It's WAY easier than that.

When you feel hurt or upset, remind yourself it's because of a belief of yours.

Don't try to figure it out, judge it, or blame others. Faulty beliefs live in the mind, so there's little point in trying to THINK your way out of it.

The BIGGEST SHIFTS happen when you STEP BACK and realize it's the thoughts themselves that are the problem.

We think we need to DO something to heal. But when you stand back and live with a little insecurity, a Band-Aid peels off a little.

YOU don't have to DO ANYTHING.

This isn't an overnight cure, but it works. Little increments add up over time.

Strong reactions get softer.

Eventually, you'll start to notice fewer worrisome thoughts.

And one day ...

... you'll feel a new sense of contentment and ease.

CHAPTER SIX

Teamwork

YOUR MIND THINKS ...

"Wow, you've said some really hard things. I feel like such a failure."

Oh no!
Your mind isn't bad.

It's the hardest little worker around,
the way it sits up there,

thinking

thinking

Thinking

all the time.

The truth is:

Left on its own,
your mind is a BAD
DECISION MAKER.

But

Working with
the rest of you,
it's a GREAT
TEAM PLAYER!

It's a question of balance. . .

When we give our MIND total control

* We feel less calm and relaxed.

* We're always thinking about the future, not living in the present.

* We can't hear
  our heart's desires.

* We crumple when something happens
  that's different from the "master plan."

Leaving our HEART in control is also not good

* We find it difficult to translate our heart's desires into the useful steps we need to finish projects.

* We have trouble working collaboratively with others.

* We forget to feed the dog, change our underpants, or pay the phone bill.

You want your HEART to be POWERFUL

AND

You want your MIND to be POWERFUL too.

You don't want your mind to overpower your heart since your heart is where your wisdom lies.

Want to know the easiest way to hear the wisdom in your heart and get your heart and mind working as a team?

Yes! Doing NOTHING allows the wisdom of your heart to bubble-up.

Doing Nothing means NOT:

* Reading or writing
* Talking to your friends
* Paying bills
* Watching television
* Cleaning your room!! (Yay doing nothing)
* Updating your status to tell everyone you're doing nothing

Let your mind run, like a child playing.

Notice what it's up to from time to time, if you're inclined. But it's not necessary.

Your mind might talk more loudly—which is common—and tell you to get up and do something. Or it might be quiet.

However it is for you is perfect. There is no right or wrong way to do it!

Doing nothing, letting your mind wander, is a type of meditation.

But you can!

Anyone can do it. And you can do it anywhere. You don't even have to be somewhere quiet.

You can do nothing for a SHORT TIME— like 10 seconds or 5 minutes;

a MEDIUM TIME—like 30 minutes or 2 hours;

or a LONGER TIME—like a day or a week.

It all depends on the reboot you need. But don't underestimate the power of 15 minutes of DOING NOTHING sprinkled through your day.

Doing nothing is one of the most productive things you can do.

The silence unlocks your wise inner voice, and your mind keeps everything on track.

You still have your mind to help you edit your assignments and get to work on time...

But now you GET IDEAS.

You FEEL what the right thing to do is.

And when you connect with your heart, it's easy to feel motivated!

Your mind isn't always going to like it. But try it. Start small.

Well, I just think you should be doing something. Like today's crossword. You haven't done it yet.

ATTENTION OVERACHIEVERS:

This isn't a competition.
If it gets too intense, stop.
You'll gain more by trying less.

Give yourself a chance to connect with YOU. The bit of you that knows who you really are.

The bit of you without insecurities and hang-ups.

Artists know the power of DOING NOTHING.

They do the work. But they also take long lazy breaks. They know the truly inspired work doesn't come from their mind alone.

Acceptance

YOUR MIND THINKS ...

How am I ever going to get all this together?

WHEN REALLY ...

Well, you're not doing anything wrong.

It's easy to think, "Oh wow, I need to do everything the book says."

Or, "I want to be calm all the time like other people are."

Ha ha ha ha ha ha ha ha ha ha ha ha ha
ha ha ha ha ha ha ha ha ha ha ha ha ha
ha ha ha ha ha ha ha ha ha ha ha ha ha
ha ha ha ha ha ha ha ha ha ha ha ha ha
ha ha ha ha ha ha ha ha ha ha ha ha ha
ha ha ha ha ha ha ha ha ha ha ha ha ha
ha ha ha ha ha ha ha ha ha ha ha ha ha
ha ha ha ha ha ha ha ha ha ha ha ha ha
ha ha ha ha ha ha ha ha ha ha ha ha ha
ha ha ha ha ha ha ha ha ha ha ha ha ha
ha ha ha ha ha ha ha ha ha ha ha ha ha
ha ha ha ha ha ha ha ha ha ha ha ha ha
ha ha ha ha ha ha ha ha ha ha ha ha ha
ha ha ha ha ha ha ha ha ha ha.

That's how funny it is thinking other people are calm all the time.

The REAL TRICK to feeling OK, even when times are tough is ...

ACCEPTANCE

It's all about
DIGGING YOUR
SELF.

But I worry a lot. And I'm negative and bossy. It's confusing, if I accept myself it means it's OK being bossy. It would be much easier to dig me when I'm not bossy anymore.

THAT'S YOUR MIND TALKING!

And getting all fixated on how you'll be in the future, which never comes.

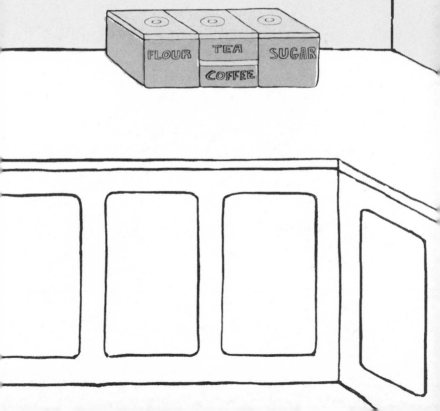

TAKE **Negativity**

You might be full of negative thoughts,*

So what!!?

You're not doing anything wrong.
Negative thoughts are natural.

And anyway, you probably won't always
have so many. You just do right now.

*You're not alone.

OR CONFUSION

That's not a big deal either.

Confusion is part of learning.

The discombobulation you feel as you consider a genuinely new idea is a normal first step toward change.

Confused a lot? It could be you're learning a lot.

Relax. Give it time.

And worrying and being judgmental is what the mind does.

All those things you regret? We all have them. They're a normal part of life.

Accepting where you are,
however you are,
is simply
the most Loving
and Compassionate
thing you can do

The TRICK to Acceptance is to KEEP LAYERING it ON.

(It's easy to stop too soon.)

Notice your inclination to be bossy or rigid (or whatever), and accept that.

Notice how you are hard on yourself, and accept that too.

And if you forget to be accepting— Yup, accept this too!

It's all OK!

Acceptance is a pile of blankets.
GRAB AS MANY AS YOU NEED.

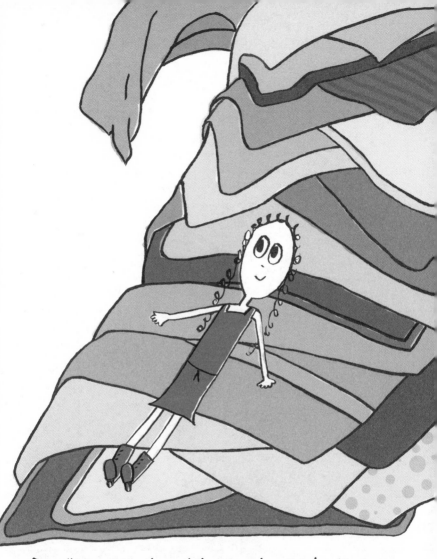

Don't worry about being buried alive in blankets. Another name for acceptance ... is LOVE.

If the house is a shambles, you haven't left the couch in days, and you can't talk without crying, who's to say that's not the perfect reaction?

Living and growing and healing isn't some shiny thing.

Sometimes it's messy.

We have an idea that we need to become a better version of ourselves.

But this is just another mind trick.

You are already the best and only version of you. You just have trouble seeing it.

You may do incredible things.
You may do non-incredible things.
But these aren't who YOU are.

Underneath all your THOUGHTS,
Underneath all your EMOTIONS,
underneath all the THINGS YOU DO,
you're already
    WHOLE and COMPLETE.

Right now, sitting here, reading this,
YOU are already everything.

It might not seem like it sometimes.

But you are.

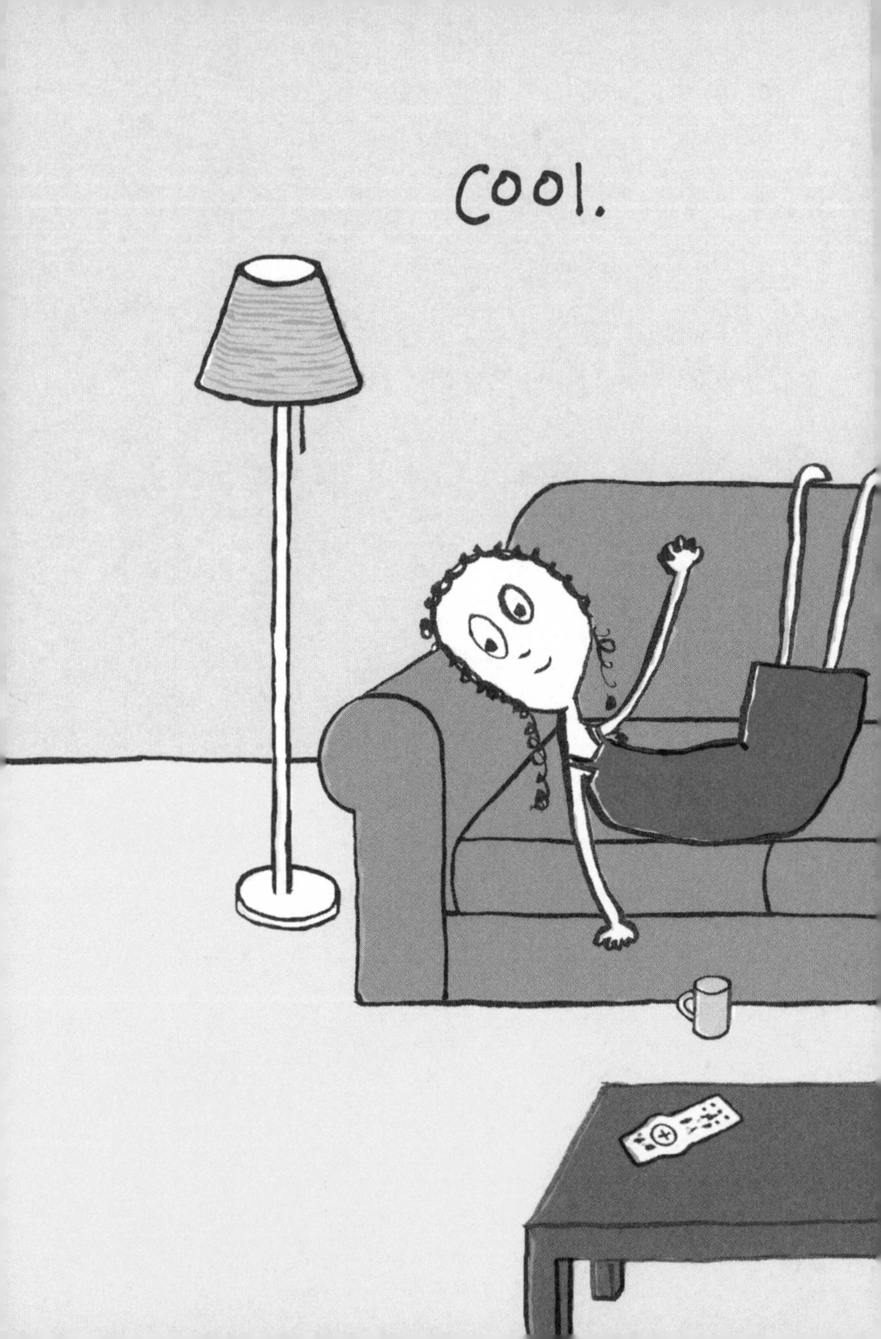
COOL.

THE END

With special thanks to

Don Morrison, Dr. Ken Manning,
Shar Cullinane, Suzanne Nelson,
Steve Harris, Lauren Appleton,
John Duff, Dr. Amy Johnson,
Karen Frank, and friends, family,
and readers of the original ebook.

AUTHOR PHOTO

Lisa & Franco Esile
("Ay-zee-Lay.")

Lisa and Franco live in Los Angeles. Lisa is from New Zealand and Franco is from New England. Both have been places and done things, but mostly they just go to the supermarket or for a bike ride or out to play music.

Visit them at francoandlisa.com. They have a free book for you.